D0606297

The Skateboarder's Guide to
Skate Parks, Half-Pipes, Bowls, and Obstacles ™

DREAM BUILDERS

The World's Best Skate Park Creators

Justin Hocking

rosen central™

., New York

For Matt and Sean

Published in 2005 by The Rosen Publishing Group, Inc.
29 East 21st Street, New York, NY 10010

First Edition

Library of Congress Cataloging-in-Publication Data

Hocking, Justin.
Dream builders: the world's best skate park creators/Justin Hocking.
   p. cm.—(The skateboarder's guide to skate parks, half-pipes, bowls,
   and obstacles)
Includes bibliographical references and index.
ISBN 1-4042-0338-9 (library binding)
1. Skateboarding parks—United States—Design and construction.
I. Title. II. Series: Hocking, Justin. Skateboarder's guide to skateboard
parks, half-pipes, bowls, and other obstacles.
GV859.8.H612 2004
796.22—dc22

2004008557

Manufactured in the United States of America

On the cover: Construction of an outdoor concrete skate park

CONTENTS

INTRODUCTION

If you're interested in skateboarding, then you probably already know a little bit about skate parks. Maybe you've seen professional skaters like Jamie Thomas or Elissa Steamer skating them on TV, in videos, and even in video games. Or, if you like to skateboard yourself, maybe you hit your local skate park every day after school. Either way, the chances are good that you already know just how much fun these cement and wooden wonderlands can be.

Professional skaters like Elissa Steamer, shown here, practice at skate parks.

What you might not know, though, is that skateboard parks have been around for a long time. In fact, the first parks were built more than thirty years ago in places such as Carlsbad, California; Port Orange, Florida; and Honolulu, Hawaii. However, as skateboarding went through several peaks and valleys of popularity, so did skate parks themselves, and all of these early masterpieces were eventually destroyed.

Fortunately, skateboarding has reached a more steady level of popularity and acceptance in the past ten years. There are now an estimated 10 million skateboarders in the United States, and professional skateboarders such as Tony Hawk, John Cardiel, and Eric Koston have become figures in the public spotlight.

This surge in the popularity of skateboarding has also helped bring about the most exciting period of skate park construction in history.

Hundreds of public skate parks have been built all over the United States in the past few years, with lots more on the way.

And as the technology and funding for these public facilities increase, a new breed of incredibly fun and functional skate parks is cropping up all over the country. If riding parks is your passion, it's a great time to be a skateboarder.

With the huge increase in demand for public skate terrain, a handful of highly specialized skate park construction companies have formed. Unlike the average construction crew that has no experience with skateboarding, these custom crews are dedicated to building nothing but the finest skate parks. This focus is what allows them to construct the most creative and highly functional skate terrains ever built.

This book is all about these highly specialized workers, the world's best custom skate park builders and designers, and the insane skate dreamscapes they create. We'll also talk about some basics of skate park construction and give you some tips for getting involved in this growing field.

CHAPTER 1

Dreamland Skateparks

E very summer, hundreds of skateboarders hit the road and head to the state of Oregon. Some come to get a break from scorching weather in places like California or Arizona and to enjoy all the natural wonders that the Pacific Northwest has to offer: misty rain forests, glacier-capped volcanoes, and beautiful sandy beaches. Professional skaters like Tony Hawk and Danny Way sometimes show up and put on public skate demonstrations for huge crowds of fans. But ask any of these wandering skaters why they're really there, and most of them will give you the same answer: to skate in the skate parks built by Dreamland.

Based out of Lincoln City, Oregon, Dreamland Skateparks is considered the finest and most experienced cement skate park construction company in the world. And along with the parks it has built all up and down Oregon, it has also constructed epic skate parks in Idaho, Montana, Indiana, Arkansas, and even as far away as Rattenberg, Austria.

Dreamland's History

In the early 1990s, the skateboarding industry hit a slump. Major skate companies that had thrived during an industry boom in the late 1980s were now going out of business.

As the popularity of skateboarding faded briefly, dedicated skaters found themselves with fewer and fewer legal places to ride. Fed up with getting hassled by police and receiving tickets for doing what they loved best, skaters in Portland, Oregon, decided to take action.

Mark "Red" Scott performs a trick called a frontside air in one of the bowls designed by Dreamland. Some of the best skateboarders in the world have come to Dreamland skate parks.

Headed by local legendary skateboarders such as Mark "Red" Scott and Sage Bolyard, the skaters of Portland began constructing their own makeshift skate park below the Burnside Bridge. With absolutely no money from the city and an all-volunteer labor force, the Burnside Skate Park, as the park came to be known, began to slowly take shape. What started out as a small assortment of banks, quarter-pipes, and bowls soon grew into what many skaters consider the most famous skate park in the world, a place where skaters from all over the country and the world come to ride.

At first, the city government of Portland was less than supportive of this grassroots project, and it even threatened to bulldoze the place on several occasions. But the Burnside project has persisted and evolved, as

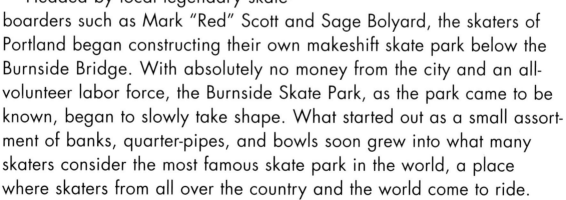

7

have the skaters who built it. In fact, using the experience they gained from building Burnside, Mark Scott and Sage Bolyard, along with several others, went on to form Dreamland Skateparks, one of the most sought-after skate park designers and builders in the world.

How Dreamland Does It

What makes Dreamland Skateparks so amazingly good? The main reason is that the company believes that skateboarders should build skate parks. Skate parks are different from plain old sidewalks, and the Dreamland crew understands that it takes a skateboarder's eye and experience to make a skate park that is both creative and highly functional.

Dreamland builds skate parks using a model it calls the design/build process. Usually, when a city government builds a public playground or park, it hires an architect to do the design work. Then a construction crew is hired to actually build the park, using the architect's blueprints as a guideline. This process works for many projects, but skate parks are different.

When a city hires Dreamland to build a park, Dreamland gets a company that does both the design and the construction. That way, Dreamland controls the whole process, leaving less room for mistakes or miscommunication that could occur between regular architects and construction crews, which usually have no experience with skating or building a skate park. The design/build process also ensures that actual skateboarders are involved in every step.

The folks at Dreamland also believe that the local skaters should play a part in designing their skate park, since they're the ones who'll be riding it the most. Whenever Dreamland travels to a new town for a building project, it holds meetings with the local skateboarders, giving them a chance to explain what sort of features they'd like to see at the

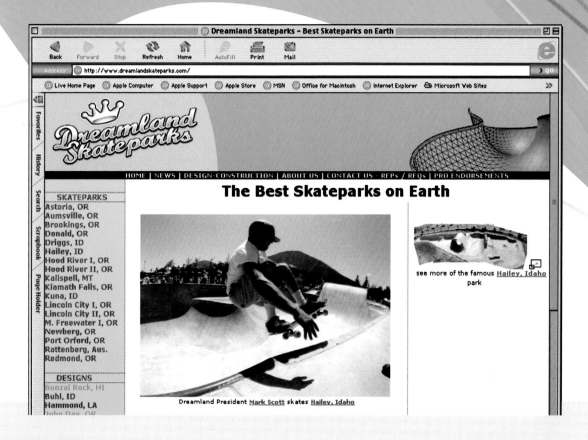

The Dreamland Web site gives you a complete tour of its offerings and where to write for brochures and information packets, as well as links to all its skate parks nationwide.

park. These ideas are then incorporated into the final design by Dreamland designers.

As the actual construction process begins, Dreamland's crew begins shaping and digging to create a rough form of the park. Crew members use shovels and excavators, which are special vehicles with adjustable plows on the front designed to move large amounts of earth.

As the park begins to take shape, Dreamland's president, Mark Scott, constantly reevaluates the original design, making small changes based on his experienced skateboarder's intuition about what will make the most functional and fun final product.

A VERY SHORT LESSON IN SHOTCRETE

Creating a flat section of concrete sidewalk is relatively simple. After workers build some molds out of wood and rebar, they pour concrete from a large cement mixing truck via a long tube. Then, using flat tools called trowels, the workers smooth the cement out, similar to smoothing butter on toast with a knife.

On the other hand, the process for building a smooth, vertically curving section of a skate park is a lot more complicated. To form a quarter-pipe or bowl wall, builders use a special concrete called shotcrete. Rather than being poured out of a tube or a wheelbarrow, shotcrete actually gets "shot" out of a high-pressure hose, similar to the hoses firefighters use to put out fires. This allows concrete workers to spray the cement high up onto the transition. Then workers climb curved ladders and smooth the cement out using specially shaped trowels along with a long curved tool called a scree. Once the concrete has been shaped and troweled, it takes a couple of days to dry and fully harden. After everything's all dry and smooth, it's skate time!

Once it has dug out and built up the soil to make a basic form of the park, the Dream Team, as the crew is called, then lays out metal rods, called rebar, in a complex grid. Like the bones beneath your skin, rebar is a sort of metal skeleton that gives strength to concrete.

Once the rebar is done, the crew sets the coping, which is the round pipe at the top of each transition that skaters use for tricks called grinds and slides. After this is all finished, a special kind of concrete called shotcrete is sprayed over the rebar to create the curving sections of the park.

Sounds sort of simple, right? The process is a lot more complicated than it might seem, and it takes a lot of experience, precise calculations, and extremely hard labor to get everything right.

Since it opened, Dreamland's Lincoln City Skate Park has received rave reviews from pro skaters as well as from local skaters. Above is one of the park's sections featuring several obstacles, pyramids, and bowls.

Lincoln City Skate Park

Located on the rugged, tree-lined coast of Oregon, Dreamland's Lincoln City Skate Park is another gem. Divided in two sections, the original upper section was completed in 1999 and named the Gnarliest Skate Park in America by *Thrasher* magazine.

A second section was completed in 2002, and consists of a tight bowl complex system and a small street section under a large open-air shelter, which comes in very handy in western Oregon, where it rains about half the year. This section, also called Phase II, contains one of the gnarliest features ever built, the Cradle. Imagine a gigantic, 20-foot-high (6.1 m) cereal bowl balanced vertically on its edge, and you'll have an idea of what the Cradle's all about. The Cradle is definitely for experts

11

only, and it allows a few fearless skaters to go almost completely upside down on their boards.

Newberg Skate Park

While the Dreamland crew has completed more than twenty-four world-class facilities, its most famous park at this point is located in Newberg, Oregon, a suburb of Portland. At almost 30,000 square feet (2,787 sq. m), Newberg Skate Park is one of the largest outdoor cement parks in the world.

But it's not just size that makes Newberg great. The Dreamland crew is famous for pouring ultra-smooth, seamless sections of concrete. You can ride Newberg for hours and never hit a single kink. Newberg's greatness owes also to its incredible design, which incorporates a series of linked bowls, banks, hips, pump bumps, pyramids, snake runs, and ledges. In just one run, it's possible to carve a gigantic bowl, grind an 11-foot-tall (3.4 m) vert wall, catch air over a hip, pump through a snake run, and then hit a grindbar shaped like a dragon.

And if you have the energy, that's only the beginning of what's possible at this concrete wonderland. But don't just take it from us— Newberg gets props from everyone who shows up. Tony Hawk, one of the best skaters ever, said it has the "best cement contours I've ever ridden, by far," according to the Dreamland website. And on a scale from one to ten, *Thrasher* magazine rated Newberg an eleven!

Newberg also contains a couple of completely unique obstacles that you won't find anywhere else. One of these, known by many as "the spinning volcano of death," is in the shape of a small volcano with transitions all the way around the base approximately 3.5 feet (1 m) high. On top of the volcano is a metal cylinder that actually rotates. A few brave skaters can ride up the volcano, stall on the cylinder, and actually spin around before rolling back down.

DREAM TEAM SPOTLIGHT: SAGE BOLYARD

Dreamland employs only die-hard skateboarders, and Sage Bolyard is one of them. As an amateur skateboarder, he is endorsed by companies such as Vans Shoes, Independent Truck Co., Spitfire Wheels, Adidas, and MM Skateboards. And he's more than earned his success. He's been skateboarding longer than most young skaters have even been alive—twenty-two years, to be exact. When Bolyard isn't designing a new Dreamland park (so far he's helped design and build sixteen of them), he can usually be found skating at Burnside Skate Park, the proving ground where he first learned his world-class concrete shaping skills.

Hailey Skate Park

Measuring in at 12,500 square feet (1,161 sq. m), Dreamland's Hailey Skate Park in Hailey, Idaho, covers a much smaller space than Newberg or Lincoln City. But what it lacks in size, it makes up for in sheer gnarliness.

The park looks like one large, complex in-ground swimming pool, with a small snake run, a more street-oriented section at the top, and a gigantic 13-foot-deep (4 m) bowl at the bottom. But what you find in between those sections is what gives Hailey its originality and scariness: a 16-foot-tall (4.9 m) "full-pipe," which is basically a huge concrete tube.

And, if that isn't scary enough, the park is designed so that you can actually roll over the top of the full-pipe. Your stomach drops as you float

Hailey Skate Park in Idaho *(above)* has been in multiple skateboarding videos and is the topic of a widely popular skateboarding movie *Northwest*, which came out in 2003.

up the full-pipe's peak. And rolling down the back side is like the first drop on a roller coaster, shooting you into the deep bowl at speeds of up to 20 miles per hour (32.2 km/h) .

CHAPTER 2

Grindline

few hours north of Seattle, you can board a ferryboat bound for the scenic San Juan Islands off the coast of Washington. As the ship leaves port, you glide through the huge body of water known as Puget Sound, where it's not uncommon to spot sea lions and killer whales.

After a few minutes at sea, the islands come into view, with their thick forests, cliff formations, and rolling hills. If you get off the ferry at Orcas Island ("orcas" is another name for killer whales), you can find something you might not expect: one of the best concrete skate parks in the world. It might seem strange to find a world-class skate park on a small, sparsely populated island, but its presence there is all thanks to the skate park company Grindline.

Grindline is based in Seattle, and its employees are seen as true masters of concrete skate park construction.

At left is the Rotary Skate Park in Bainbridge Island, Washington, which extends for 14,000 square feet (1,301 sq. m). At right is the Scott Stamnes Memorial Skate Park in Orcas Island, Washington, which was named for a skater who was killed in a drunk driving accident.

The company is known for building deep pools with interesting free-form shapes (shapes that are unique to each particular skate park) and tons of hips. Grindline is also at the forefront of modern street course designs in places such as Wolfpoint, Montana.

Grindline skate parks are found mostly in the state of Washington, but the company has also built parks in Colorado, Oregon, Montana, Ohio, and North Carolina, and it has helped with designs in places as far away as Okinawa, Japan.

The History of Grindline Skate Parks

Grindline is owned and operated by skate legend Mark Hubbard, also known as Monk. Monk helped in the construction of Burnside Skate Park in Portland, Oregon. But he lived about three hours north of Portland, in

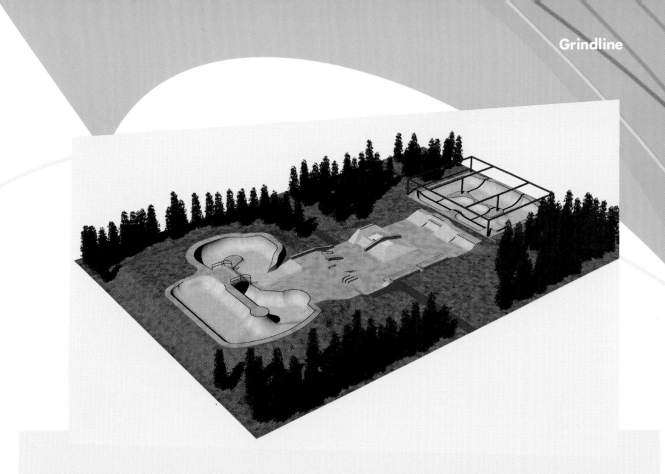

Above is a Grindline park design to be built in Anchorage, Alaska. It will measure 25,000 square feet (2,323 sq. m), and will feature a full-pipe and a street course.

Seattle. Fed up with having no place to skate, Hubbard began building swimming pools for a living. With the knowledge he gained from this experience, he started shaping concrete skate pools in his friend's backyard. And drawing on that experience, he eventually started Grindline. His company has built more than fifty parks and definitely has one of the best reputations in the business.

How Grindline Does It

After getting a contract to build a new park, the first stage in the process for Grindline is meeting with local skaters. The Grindline

Grindline uses a design/build process when creating its parks. The company designs with the input of local skaters and then starts the construction process. This involves laying rebar, or the metal bars shown here. The rebar supports the concrete, which will be applied in the next phase of construction.

design specialists listen to the local skaters' ideas about what they would like to see in a skate park, and then they incorporate their own experience to create a rough plan for the park. This plan usually goes through several revisions, and then a three-dimensional computerized blueprint is created with a special computer program called Rhino. This allows the Grindline team and the local skaters to take a virtual tour of the future park before it's even built, which gives them a chance to make changes and correct mistakes.

Once the building phase begins, Grindline uses a design/build philosophy similar to Dreamland's. This allows the company to be flexible, and if problems exist in the design, the crew works them out as it goes. One difference between Grindline and Dreamland is that Grindline often incorporates concrete pool coping (the same kind of concrete ledge that you find on the edge of backyard swimming pools) into its bowls, rather than metal coping, which gives all Grindline parks a unique rugged feel.

Scott Stamnes Memorial Skate Park

Grindline's Scott Stamnes Memorial Skate Park in Orcas Island, Washington, was built to commemorate legendary Pacific Northwest skateboarder Scott Stamnes. This 20,000-square-foot (1,858 sq. m) island park is filled with just about every obstacle imaginable, including an actual island. That's right, at the center of this epic park, you'll find something you won't see just about anywhere else in the world: a very large circular bowl with a concrete island in the middle. This section of the park is the most challenging, with steep transitions, walls as high as 10 feet (3 m) tall, a roll-in, and a treacherous obstacle known as the death box.

Surrounding the island bowl is something like a concrete bobsled course, with steeply curving inverted walls. This allows skaters to roll around the perimeter of the park in continuous circles, hitting small hips, ledges, and bumps along the way.

CHAPTER 3

Team Pain

Imagine this scene: world champion skateboarder Tony Hawk gets ready to drop in on a perfect vert ramp while thousands of fans cheer him on from below. Some of his best friends and fellow pro skateboarders Bob Burnquist, Andy MacDonald, and Bucky Lasek, smack their skateboards on the coping in a thunderous show of support, as is the custom. With his heart racing, Hawk drops in. On the other side of the ramp, he does an air, launches well over head height above the deck, and spins a full two and a half rotations, or 900 degrees, in the air. When he lands and rides away, the crowd goes completely berserk, and Hawk walks away with a new world record for being the first person to land the trick.

This was the actual scene at the 1999 Summer X Games, an extreme sports competition, in San Francisco, California. The X Games is a popular event, watched by millions of spectators. But while most people might recognize Tony Hawk or Bob Burnquist, they have no idea who actually built the ramps for these contests.

The majority of the X Games facilities are built by a crew called Team Pain, headed by legendary skate park builder Tim Payne. While Dreamland and Grindline are known for building the epic concrete parks, Tim Payne, who also builds incredible wooden ramps and parks, is acknowledged as the one of the best all-around skate park builders in the world. With four full-time crews—two for concrete and two for wood—Team Pain is also one of the largest of all the skate park construction companies.

The History of Team Pain

In 1986, the skateboard company Powell Peralta released *The Search for Animal Chin*, one of the most creative and entertaining skateboarding movies ever made. In the film, a group of legendary skaters known as the Bones Brigade sets out on an epic quest to find a mysterious master skateboarder named Animal Chin.

The brigade was made up of skate heroes Tony Hawk, Steve Caballero, Lance Mountain, Mike McGill, and Tommy Guerrero. Their search brought them to famous skate spots such as the Wallows Ditch in Hawaii, Lance Mountain's backyard vert ramp, and a famous pool at the Pink Motel in Southern California.

In the final scene, the Bones Brigade discovers a giant vert ramp, the likes of which had never been seen before. Called the Chin Ramp, it actually has two half-pipe sections connected together, as well as tombstone extensions, a mini-half-pipe built on the deck, and an actual tunnel that connects two sections of the complex ramp.

The movie's finale includes footage of the Bones Brigade skaters skating this ramp, taking incredible lines, and doing runs with two, three, and four

At left is a full-pipe under construction that was later featured in a Disney commercial starring Tony Hawk. At right is the Team Pain crew, which has built more than 200 skate parks.

skaters riding the ramp at the same time. It was some of the most exhilarating skateboarding footage ever seen or imagined.

The famous and incredibly innovative Chin Ramp was built by Tim Payne. At that point he'd been building backyard ramps all over the East Coast and was also the head builder for the National Skateboard Association (NSA), an organization that set up contests popular in the 1980s.

But completing the Chin Ramp was the feat that truly launched Payne's career. His business took off in the 1990s, leading him to hire several teams of builders, all called Team Pain. And all this teamwork has paid off. Tim Payne and Team Pain have built more than 200 world-class skateboard facilities and have won several awards, including *Thrasher* magazine's award for Best Skate Park, as well as a 2002 Merit Award for Design by the American Society of Landscape Architects.

How Team Pain Does It

All the Team Pain crews are made up of skateboarders with at least fifteen years of experience. Since Team Pain builds several types of custom skate parks, the crew members have many different skills, including carpentry, excavation, cement masonry, and welding.

While all of Team Pain's projects are different, each is finished using the design/build method, similar to that of Dreamland and Grindline. This means that Team Pain designs and builds all of its skate parks, instead of just building parks designed by an outside architect. This method also allows Team Pain to begin basic construction of the skate park before the actual plans are finalized. This saves valuable time and money, and allows for creative design solutions.

Team Pain builds three different categories of custom skate parks and ramps: outdoor concrete parks, indoor wooden parks, and high-profile ramps for professionals.

Rio Grande Skate Park

Located high in the rugged Rocky Mountains, the town of Aspen, Colorado, is known for its incredible wintertime skiing and snowboarding. It's a popular summertime destination, too, as many tourists come to hike, swim, ride horses—and skateboard. There's not much street skating in such a small mountain town, but you will find the outdoor cement masterpiece known as the Rio Grande Skate Park.

One of Team Pain's finest creations, the Rio Grande Skate Park, was voted the Best Skate Park in Colorado by *Thrasher* magazine, which is no small accomplishment in a state known for its abundance of quality skate parks. What makes it so good? The Rio Grande Skate Park has some of the smoothest concrete ever poured. In fact, some skaters complain that its glassy surface is almost too smooth. With such a glossy finish, a common problem is that bright sunlight reflects off the concrete, making it difficult for skaters to see. To solve this problem, Team Pain put a reddish brown dye in the concrete mix. The earth tone also helps the park blend in with its natural surroundings.

The Rio Grande Skate Park measures 17,000 square feet (1,579 sq. m). The main section consists of several small bowls connected by spines and hips. There's also a 2-foot-deep (0.6 m) micro-pool, which is smaller than a traditional pool. It's the perfect place for beginners to learn how to drop in.

There are also some more street-oriented obstacles in the park, including some ledges and a flat bar to do grinds and slides on. For more advanced skaters, there's a large bowl shaped like a four-leaf clover (also known as a clover bowl), with a 10-foot (3 m) deep end.

Woodward Skateboard Camp

With seven huge indoor skateboard facilities and six outdoor skate areas, all totaling well over 100,000 square feet (9,290 sq. m) of skateboard terrain, Woodward Skateboard Camp, an indoor wooden park, in Woodward, Pennsylvania, and an outdoor park in Stallion Springs, California, is by far the largest skateboard facility in the world.

In 2000, the owners of this incredible summer camp hired Team Pain to build a huge concrete bowl complex known as the Rock, with 20,000 square feet (1,858 sq. m) of bowls, pools, wedges, ledges, rails, spines, hips, and much more.

At top is the construction of Woodward West in Stallion Springs, California, a West Coast branch of the Woodward Skateboard Camp in Woodward, Pennsylvania. Inset, a skater enjoys one of the completed Woodward West's outdoor concrete obstacles.

Skatelab Indoor Skate Park and Museum

Located north of Los Angeles in Simi Valley, California, Skatelab is one of the most famous indoor wooden skate parks in the country. Originally designed by Team Pain, the park has two large street course areas with tons of quarter-pipes, ledges, and rails.

The Skatelab has another claim to fame: it's home to the world's first and largest skateboard museum, where you can find more than 2,000 vintage skateboards on display, along with all sorts of cool

Bob Burnquist's backyard ramp *(above)* in San Diego, California, is better than some of those found in municipal skate parks. It features an "oververt" bowl section, which can be seen at the far end.

skate memorabilia like T-shirts, hats, and stickers. More than 25,000 people visit every year to find out about the radical and colorful history of skateboarding.

Bob Burnquist's Ramp

Back in the 1980s, it was common for skaters across the country to build large vert half-pipes in their backyards. Known simply as backyard ramps, they provided a great place for skaters to hang out and skate (and barbecue!). But in the early 1990s, as the popularity of vertical skateboarding declined, most backyard ramps disappeared.

26

Fortunately, vertical skating made a comeback in the mid-1990s, thanks mainly to professional skaters like Bob Burnquist. One of the top vert skaters in the world, Burnquist is famous for inventing highly technical and innovative tricks, and also for doing entire runs while riding switch (which means he stands in the opposite stance on the board).

After purchasing a house in the dry, rolling hills east of San Diego, California, Burnquist decided to bring back the backyard ramp. He hired Team Pain to build the ultimate ramp—one of the biggest half-pipes ever built—complete with an "oververt" bowl section, which is similar to a wooden version of the Cradle at the Lincoln City Skate Park. Bob's ramp is so big and cool that it's even been called the New Millennial Chin Ramp—a nod to the famous ramp that originally launched Tim Payne's successful career.

CHAPTER 4

Site Design Group

When he was twelve years old, Mike McIntyre built a miniramp in the backyard of his family's home in California. It was there that he developed his love for building and designing skateboard ramps and parks. A few years later, when he was fifteen, he was ready for something bigger and better, so he built a full-sized vert ramp that local skaters eventually named Page Mill Ramp. On most weekends, twenty to thirty skaters would come from all over the state to session, or skate, the ramp, including soon-to-be skate gods Tony Hawk and Steve Caballero.

After graduating from high school, McIntyre earned a bachelor's degree in landscape design from California Polytechnic State University in San Luis Obispo, California. He then moved to Phoenix, Arizona, where he began working for a large architectural firm.

Fortunately, he came to the right place at the right time. As of 1990, there weren't any public skate parks in the Phoenix area, but the increasing popularity of skateboarding fueled an explosion in the demand for parks. McIntyre designed several parks, and when his phone began ringing off the hook from people asking for his help with other parks, he quit his job and founded his own company, Site Design Group.

Widely acknowledged as one of the best park designers in the southwestern United States and the world, McIntyre and his large crew have designed more than seventy-six parks in Arizona, California, Colorado, Utah, and Texas. But they've also started branching out of the Southwest to states such as Oregon, Illinois, Hawaii, Kentucky, and North Carolina. McIntyre also designed a Tony Hawk signature skate park (one that Tony Hawk helped design, approve, and fund) in Durban, South Africa. From a small backyard ramp in California to a world-class park in South Africa two decades later, McIntyre and the Site crew have definitely come a long way.

How Site Design Group Does It

Unlike companies like Dreamland and Grindline that use the design/build method, Site Design Group focuses mainly on designing parks and then uses its construction branch, Site Skate Parks, to actually build the parks. This allows it to focus exclusively on creating unique and highly functional skate park designs. And, like most other companies, Site understands the importance of letting actual skateboarders design parks. Everyone on the staff has years of skateboarding experience. During the design phase, the company holds public meetings with local skaters so that the people who will actually skate the park get to have a say in how it will look.

Just because the skateboarders who run Site don't actually have a hand in construction doesn't mean their parks don't get built properly.

SITE TEAM MEMBER SPOTLIGHT: COLBY CARTER

One of the most important parts of professional skateboarder Colby Carter's job is skateboarding. As a professional skate park designer, it's important for him to actually test-ride all of his creations. And he's had plenty of experience doing just that.

During his twenty years of skating, he's ridden hundreds of parks all across the United States, Canada, and Europe. All this experience has taught Carter exactly what works and what doesn't work in a skate park, and this knowledge comes in handy when he sits down for a community design meeting with a group of skaters, where he's able to turn their ideas and dreams into reality. His knowledge also comes in handy when he's on an actual construction site, acting as a consultant for the construction crew.

So far, Carter has designed more than fifty public parks and sixteen private parks, while working simultaneously to finish his degree in plant biology and urban horticulture from Arizona State University.

During the construction phase, Site sends out experienced skateboarding consultants, like Colby Carter, who use their skateboarder's eye to help supervise the construction crew and make sure everything gets done right.

Wilson Skate Park

Located in a public park near downtown Chicago, Site's Wilson Skate Park has something for everyone. The large street area contains ledges, stairs, quarter-pipes, and handrails. A large intermediate bowl section in the center of the park contains different-sized quarter-pipes, hips, and

Mike McIntyre *(left)*, founder of Site Design Group, meets with pro skater Rob Dyrdek. The two collaborated on the design of the DC Shoes Skatepark in Kettering, Ohio, where Dyrdek grew up. Besides collaborating on the Kettering park, Dyrdek and DC Shoes have formed a foundation to continue building skate parks around the country.

corners, along with a small L-shaped island. The expert bowl section in the back contains a large clover bowl with concrete pool coping.

DC Shoes/Kettering Skate Park

Site's DC Shoes/Kettering Skate Park in Kettering, Ohio, is being created to look like an actual urban plaza instead of a "normal" skate park. This design, which is similar to famous street spots like Love Park in Philadelphia, was made to appeal to street skaters who would rather skate ledges, handrails, and stairs than quarter-pipes and bowls.

Above is a computer model of the proposed DC Shoes/Kettering Skate Park. DC Shoes is a well-known supplier of skateboarding shoes and other equipment and accessories to skateboarders.

The park will contain a large flat plaza in the center, with a series of staircases that extend down to a sidewalk that circles the entire park. The revolutionary 38,000-square-foot (3,530 sq. m) design also incorporates more natural elements like trees, bushes, fountains, and even sculptures to give the park the feeling of an authentic street spot.

Chandler Park

In Chandler, Arizona, one of the many suburbs of Phoenix, surrounded by tall palm trees, you can find one of the largest and best skate parks in the southwestern United States. With a good mix of street obstacles and transition, Site's Chandler Skate Park is packed with 35,000 square feet (3,252 sq. m) of perfectly shaped bowls, pyramids, manual pads, ledges, rails, and banks. With so much space and so many different obstacles, Chandler Skate Park has something for all skaters—beginner, intermediate, or expert. Chandler's system of bright stadium lights also allows skaters to ride at night and avoid Phoenix's scorching daytime temperatures.

CHAPTER 5

Wally Hollyday Designs and RCMC Custom Cement Parks

When he was nineteen years old, young Wally Hollyday got a job helping build a skate park called Cherry Hill near his hometown in New Jersey. It was 1978, and Hollyday had no formal training with concrete. The only real experience he had with skate parks was riding them.

But Wally was a hard worker with a good eye for building smooth concrete curves. He proved himself on the work site, digging many of the transitions by hand. In the end, he and the pool-building crew that hired him created 34,000 square feet (3,159 sq. m) of radical indoor terrain, including the legendary Eggbowl, in Cherry Hill, New Jersey. Named for its egglike shape, the Eggbowl was, at that time, considered to be the finest skateboard pool ever built.

Cherry Hill was home to pro Shogo Kubo, a pool-skating legend known for his incredible surf-influenced style. As it had for Kubo, Cherry Hill also made Hollyday a legend, not for his skateboarding, but for his perfectionist skate park construction skills.

Hollyday went on to build several more parks in the 1970s, including Apple Skate Park in Ohio. Unfortunately, the popularity of skateboarding faded in the early 1980s, and many skate parks—including the Cherry Hill park—were destroyed. With no more parks to build, Hollyday was understandably disappointed, but he went on to pursue other personal projects such as photography.

Twenty years later, as skate park construction began to boom again, Hollyday fortunately got back into the business. He now manages his own company, Wally Hollyday Designs, and works with another company called California Skate Parks. Business is booming again for Hollyday. He's now designed and helped build more than forty parks.

Owl's Head

The Big Apple, otherwise known as New York City, might seem like an unlikely place for a world-class skate park. But New York City has a thriving skate scene, especially after the addition of a public skate park in Brooklyn. With an amazing view of the famous skyscrapers of Manhattan, the Owl's Head Skate Park has both wooden obstacles and concrete bowls, including a kidney-shaped pool that was built with help from Hollyday. This pool has a 9-foot (2.7 m) deep end and a 5-foot (1.5 m) shallow end, with concrete coping in the deep, along with Hollyday's signature smooth concrete.

RCMC Custom Cement Skate Parks

When Rick Carje was a kid growing up in the suburbs of Cleveland, Ohio, he had a dream. As a dedicated skateboarder, he spent most weekends skating the celebrated parks built by Wally Hollyday, such as Apple Skate Park in Columbus, Ohio, or the Cherry Hill park in New Jersey. Fascinated by the perfect concrete curves he found in these dreamscape parks, Carje decided that someday he wanted to build his own skate park.

After graduating from high school, Carje moved from Ohio to New Jersey, where he got a job in a cement masonry business. Starting out at the bottom, he worked as a concrete mixer and a basic laborer. He then moved to California, where he utilized his newfound concrete skills to build custom swimming pools, fountains, and spas.

This was all during a time when few, if any, skate parks were being built. However, Carje was happy to find a few die-hard Southern California skaters building skateboard pools and bowls in their backyards. Carje helped build some of these backyard beauties, including Belmar's Pool, Chicken's Pool, and the Basic Bowl, which are often featured in skateboard videos and magazines like *Thrasher*. After returning to New Jersey, Carje worked on his first public skate park in Greenport, in Long Island, New York.

And then, in the late 1990s, as skateboarding hit another boom, Carje got a call that changed his life forever. It came from the people at Vans, a skateboard shoe company, which had decided to build a series of modern indoor skateboard facilities all over the United States. Having established a name for himself building private pools in Los Angeles, Carje was asked to head up the concrete work in all of the Vans parks. Carje stepped up to the challenge and created RCMC Custom Cement Skate Parks. Carje's original dream of someday building a skate park has definitely come true: RCMC has completed ten Vans skate parks that are widely considered to be some of the finest indoor concrete facilities in the world.

So You Want to Be a Skate Park Builder

With all the parks being built these days, skate park construction and design are good fields to get into. There are many benefits to doing this

Rick Carje's RCMC Custom Cement Skate Parks headed up the concrete construction in all of the Vans skate parks. This Vans skate park includes several interconnected bowls.

kind of work: you get to exercise your creativity, travel extensively and depending on your position, make decent money.

There are drawbacks, too, though. While you do get to build skate parks, once each one is finished, it's usually off to the next town before you get a chance to really skate it. Also, if you're working as a laborer, the work is so hard that you probably won't even have energy to skate after working all day.

If you think you'd like to get into this field some day, here are some steps you can take right now:

1. The first thing you can do is easy and fun: skate a lot of parks. Like Colby Carter, the only way to learn what works and what doesn't is to ride as many skate parks as you can.

Needles Skate Park in Needles, California, was completed in December 2003, with help from a grant from the Tony Hawk Foundation.

2. Take woodshop classes in junior high or high school to help you understand how wooden structures are built.

3. Once you turn sixteen or seventeen, try getting a job on a concrete crew. Learn the basics of how to pour concrete. You might also consider working for a carpenter and learning about woodworking.

4. If you're hoping to be more than a laborer, consider going to college to study architecture or landscape design. Having a college degree gives you many opportunities and will help if you'd like to start your own skate park construction company.

5. Build some of your own skateboard obstacles at home. If you have the time and money (and your parents' permission), try building a mini-half-pipe in your backyard. You can use our book *Awesome Obstacles: How to Build Your Own Skateboard Ramps and Ledges*, also part of this series, as a reference.

6. If a skate park is being built in your neighborhood, try to get involved. (Check out *Taking Action: How to Get Your City to Build a Public Skate Park*, another book in this series, for tips on how to get a public park in your town.) Offer to volunteer your labor on the construction site. You might be asked to just pick up trash, but it's a good chance to be around a site and see how things work.

GLOSSARY

bank A steep slope, or embankment, usually made out of concrete.

bowl A special type of skate structure that's shaped like a giant bowl. There are several variations of bowl shapes, including clover and kidney shapes.

death box A gap at the top of a pool.

deck The flat surface at the top of a ramp or bowl where skaters wait before taking their next run.

drop in To enter a ramp from the deck.

grind A trick in which you slide on your trucks on the edge of a surface such as a ledge or a bank.

island A tall rounded pillar with transitions all around, found in the middle of a skate bowl.

ledge A short, square object used for grinds and slides.

line A series of tricks skated together in a row.

manual pad A low, flat platform that is used for manual tricks or for tricks in which you lift the front trucks up and balance on the back wheels only.

pump To flex your legs at the right spot on the transition of a ramp or pool to build up speed.

pump bump An obstacle designed to help you get extra speed by pumping over transitions.

pyramid A skate obstacle that resembles the shape of a pyramid with the top cut off.

snake run A series of long interconnected bowls that form the shape of a snake.

spine An obstacle formed when two half-pipes are connected one behind the other.

40

tombstone An extension on a ramp that gives skaters a few extra feet of height at the top. It is also known simply as an extension.

transition A word for any upward-curving skating surface.

vert ramp A ramp composed of a flat-bottom with transitions that lead to a vert, or vertical climb, on both sides.

FOR MORE INFORMATION

Dreamland Skateparks
960 Southeast Highway 101, PMB 384
Lincoln City, OR 97367-2622
(503) 577-9277
Web site: http://www.dreamlandskateparks.com

Grindline
4056 23rd Avenue SW
Seattle, WA 98106
(206) 932-6414
e-mail: inform@grindline.com
Web site: http://www.grindline.com

RCMC Custom Cement Skate Parks
48 Jefferson Road
Princeton, NJ 08540
(714) 965-1104
e-mail: carje@earthlink.net
Web site: http://www.rcmcsk8parks.com

Site Design Group, Inc.
24 W. 5th Street, Suite #203
Tempe, AZ 85281
(480) 894-6797
e-mail: info@sitedesigngroup.com
Web site: http://www.sitedesigngroup.com

Team Pain Skate Parks
890 Northern Way, Suite B-2
Winter Springs, FL 32708
(407) 366-9221
Web site: http://www.teampain.com

Web Sites

Due to the changing nature of Internet links, the Rosen Publishing Group Inc. has developed an online list of Web sites related to the subject of this book. This site is updated regularly. Please use this link to access the list:

http://www.rosenlinks.com/skgu/drbu

FOR FURTHER READING

Brooke, Michael. *The Concrete Wave: The History of Skateboarding.* Toronto, Canada: Warwick Publishing, 1999.

Davis, Garry, and Craig Steycyk. *Dysfunctional.* Corte Madera, CA: Ginkgo Press, 1999.

Doeden, Matt. *Skate Parks: Grab Your Skateboard.* Mankato, MN: Capstone Press, 2002.

Hawk, Tony. *Hawk: Occupation: Skateboarder.* New York: Reagan Books, 2000.

Thrasher Magazine. *Thrasher: Insane Terrain.* New York: Universe Publishing, 2001.

BIBLIOGRAPHY

Brooke, Michael. *The Concrete Wave: The History of Skateboarding.* Ontario, Canada: Warwick Publishing, Inc., 1999.

Buck, Ron. "1999 Summer X Games: Hawk Soars Into History with 900." Retrieved March 7, 2004 (http://espn.go.com/xgames/summerx99/skate/news/1999/990628/01329413.html).

Dreamland Skate Parks.com. "Newberg, Oregon." Retrieved March 5, 2004 (http://www.dreamlandskateparks.com/newberg.html).

Grindline.com. "Skate Parks." Retrieved March 6, 2004 (http://grindline.com/cgi-local/view.pl?view=press).

Murphy, Jim. "Dave Duncan." *Juice.* Retrieved March 16, 2004 (http://www.juicemagazine.com/dutynowrcmc1.html).

Richins, Chad. "Dude! A Gnarly Park!" Retrieved March 5, 2004 (http://www.dreamlandskateparks.com/news/news_003.html).

SiteDesignGroup.com. "Colby Carter: Skatepark Designer." Retrieved March 11, 2004 (http://www.sitedesigngroup.com/bios_colby.htm).

SiteDesignGroup.com. "Skatepark Projects." Retrieved March 11, 2004 (http://www.sitedesigngroup.com/projects.php4).

Skatelab.com. "Indoor Skatepark and Museum." Retrieved March 11, 2004 (http://www.skatelab.com/museum/index.php).

TheSidewaysGuide.com. "Aspen Skatepark." Retrieved March 11, 2004 (http://www.thesidewaysguide.com/Skate/SkateParks/States/CO/Aspen/aspenCOSPif.htm).

Woodward Camp.com "The Rock." Retrieved March 11,2004 (http://www.woodwardcamp.com/wweast/east_index.html).

INDEX

About the Author

Justin Hocking lives and skateboards in New York City. He is also an editor of the book *Life and Limb: Skateboarders Write from the Deep End*, published in 2004 by Soft Skull Press.

Credits

Cover, pp. 22, 25 (background), 25 (inset), 26 provided by Team Pain; p. 4 © AP/Wide World Photos; pp. 7, 11 © *Thrasher* Magazine; pp. 9, 14 Courtesy Dreamland Skateparks/http://www.dreamlandskateparks .com; pp. 16, 17, 18 http://www.grindline.com; pp. 31, 32 © Site Design Group, Inc./http://www. sitedesigngroup.com and Site Skateparks, Inc./http://www.siteskateparks. com; pp. 37, 38 Courtesy Wally Hollyday.

Designer: Les Kanturek; Editor: Nicholas Croce;
Photo Researcher: Rebecca Anguin-Cohen